London

Leiden

Hanover

Berlin

Frankfurt

Wrocław

Kassel

Leipzig

Dresden

Freiberg

Würzburg

Versailles

Paris

Reims

Mannheim

Regensburg

Stuttgart

Vienna

Freiburg

Ulm

Augsburg

Basel

Schaffhausen

Zürich

Bern

Lyon

Venice

Bologna

Marseille

Rome

Naples

T0085374

When a baby rhino is orphaned in India with nowhere to go, a gentle sea captain from Holland—Douwe van der Meer— decides to take her to Europe with him. Clara wins the hearts of everyone—from villagers to princes, kings, and queens who have never seen a rhino before. All are delighted by the gentle giant—whose image soon appears on posters, coins, and statuettes, until the fine day when the Dutch captain gives Clara a home of her own.

Katrin Hirt is an historian, and she lives with her family in Tübingen, Germany. In addition to her interests in scientific writing and research, she writes stories for children. *Clara the Rhino* is her first picture book.

Laura Fuchs grew up among fields and forests in North Rhine Westphalia, where there is plenty of room for people to create their own stories and pictures. Her study of illustration took her to Hamburg, where she still lives and works today. With her dog she has reached the boundaries of the city, and with her brush the hearts of the whole world.

Clara
the Rhino

Katrin Hirt • Laura Fuchs

North
South

This is a story about a rhinoceros called Clara and a time that has long since passed. In those days most people spent their entire life in a single place. They knew everything about their own home, and nothing about distant countries or unusual animals.

If these people ever did leave their homes, they would seldom travel much farther than the nearest village or town. Then they would walk or go on horseback, or drive an oxcart or ride in a stagecoach. There were no tunnels through the mountains, airplanes had not yet been invented, and the only ships were those with sails.

Nevertheless, there were merchants who would travel long distances. They would sail for months across the sea, from countries such as Holland all the way to India. There they would buy spices, coffee, and tea, and bring them back to sell in Europe.

It was at this time, almost three hundred years ago, that Clara the rhinoceros was born in India.

When she was still very small, her world was limited to the tall green grass, the moist earth, and the heavy heat. She could see the mighty figure of her mother and hear the screeching monkeys and the buzzing flies, and the cries of the birds as they flew high above her.

Then suddenly hunters arrived, and with their arrows they shot and killed her mother. But the little rhino was still alive, and the hunters picked her up and carried her away with them.

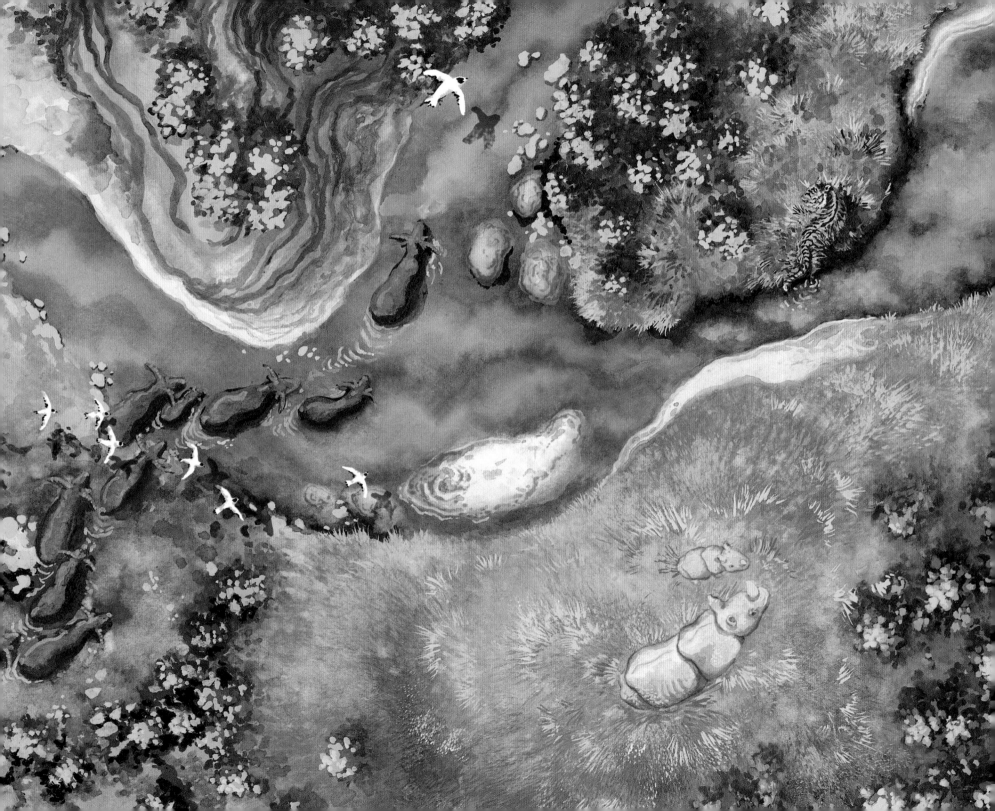

The hunters were soon eager to get rid of the little rhino, and so they took her to the nearest town and gave her to a merchant and his family. They welcomed her into their home, fed her milk, gave her a place to sleep, and called her Clara.

Clara would sniffle and snuffle around the furniture, the curtains, and the children's hands. The children would talk to her and stroke her wrinkly body, and so she lost all her fear of humans.

When the merchant invited guests for a meal, he would have the little rhino brought into the room. Then she would trot around the long table, gently nudge the guests with her nose, and eat out of the hands of the merchant's wife. The men would smile, and the ladies would clap their hands with delight.

Clara felt very much at home here. She had plenty to eat, was healthy, and grew bigger and fatter every day. Her bed was soon far too small.

In the dining room she accidentally started to knock over the furniture. The china on the table would rattle because of the sheer weight of her footsteps. Now the guests began to recoil with fear.

"This can't go on," said the merchant, shaking his head. "Clara can't stay here with us any longer."

But where was she to go? The children cried. Clara had never learned to live out in the wild. She trusted humans and would not try to run away from hunters. She had no idea what the outside world was like.

One evening a young man came to dinner. They told him about their problem and he listened carefully. His name was Douwe van der Meer. He was the captain of a merchant ship and came from Holland.

"I know what we can do!" he said. "I can solve your problem. I'll take Clara with me to Europe. Nobody there has ever seen a rhino. She'll be a sensation!"

"All right," said the merchant. "She's yours."

All the preparations for the journey were quickly made. The family went to the harbor and waved a sad good-bye to Clara as she sailed away with Captain van der Meer.

The voyage from India to Holland took many weeks. Clara's "home" was now the deck of the ship, and from there she would smell the salty air and see the horizon going up and down. She saw the sun rise in the morning and set in the evening, and she heard the sailors calling out to one another, the sails flapping in the wind, and the ever-friendly voice of Captain van der Meer.

He stayed as close as he could to Clara and told her about Holland, his home country, and about the journeys they would make together. Clara would sniff and snuffle at his coat and let him stroke her.

Douwe kept a little diary. "Clara eats 100 pounds of hay every day," he wrote. And "During the day Clara always likes to have a little snooze." He underlined this note: "Best of all Clara likes to eat oranges."

Their arrival at Rotterdam was a great event. The news spread like wildfire: "A giant animal, a real rhinoceros, has come from India!" Men and women, boys and girls came flocking to see her. They would shout, "Come here, everybody! Come and see! What a strange animal!"

Douwe van der Meer was delighted. He wanted more and more people to gaze in wonderment at Clara. And so he had a special wagon built. It had to be big and solid so that Clara could travel around in it.

He also had lots of advertisements printed, saying "A real live Indian rhinoceros is coming to your town. See her for yourself. Entry only two Groschen."

Eight horses were needed to pull Clara's wagon. It would rattle and rumble through the cobbled streets. Clara could taste the dust and hear the grinding of the wheels, the lashing whip of the coachman, and the clip-clop of the horses' hooves.

Wherever they went, people were eager to see Clara, whether young or old, rich or poor. "What a giant!" they would cry. "Look at its huge head and that dangerous horn!" Douwe would hold a measuring tape up high and ask, "Is anyone here brave enough to come and measure the rhino?"

One fearless fellow did indeed go up to Clara, measure her, and shout, "More than nine and a half feet long and over six and a half feet tall!"

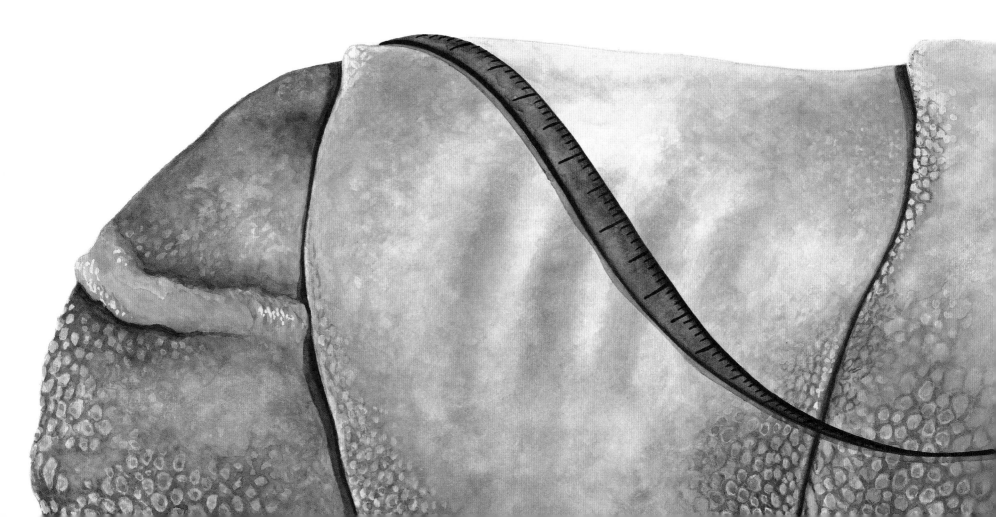

Douwe van der Meer and Clara traveled to many different countries. What fascinated the villagers and townsfolk was equally attractive to kings and queens, princes and princesses, and all the aristocrats. Dressed in their silks and satins, they and their courtiers also flocked to the city squares where Clara was on show.

"Never seen or smelt anything like it!" cried the ladies, holding their handkerchiefs to their noses.

"Remarkable!" cried the lords. And the French king Louis XV even offered to buy Clara.

But Douwe replied, "No, I'm sorry, but Clara is not for sale."

Clara was now famous. Her portrait was printed on posters and coins, and statuettes were made of her in porcelain and bronze. Newspapers published reports on her, scientists studied her, and poets wrote poems and singers sang songs about her. In Paris, fine ladies wore wigs that curved upward in the shape of a horn and were called "coiffure à la rhino."

Clara herself was very happy so long as Douwe stayed by her side. And he took great care of her, making sure that she always had a huge pile of hay and sometimes a few oranges within easy reach.

One day he said, "Let's go to the carnival in Venice." He stroked her huge head. "You will be the star attraction there!"

Douwe and Clara boarded a ship bound for Italy. But on the way there was a terrible storm. Between the waves, which were as tall as houses, the ship was raised high in the air and then flung down into the depths. Clara was hurled against the bars of her cage and roared with terror.

Douwe was busy giving orders to the sailors because as captain he knew what needed to be done.

Fortunately they all survived the storm, and no damage was done. When they reached Venice, there was already a large crowd of people, and they all cheered in celebration of Clara's arrival.

They knew that the great rhino had only just escaped from the dangers of the sea and so she now seemed even more precious. They hung garlands of flowers over her and gave her sweet fruits to eat. There was even a famous artist who came and painted her portrait.

Clara accepted all this with great patience, but Douwe could sense that his dear friend was now exhausted. One day when he was alone with her, he whispered, "We've traveled long and far enough. Now you and I need a home of our own." Clara nuzzled him and rubbed her head against his coat.

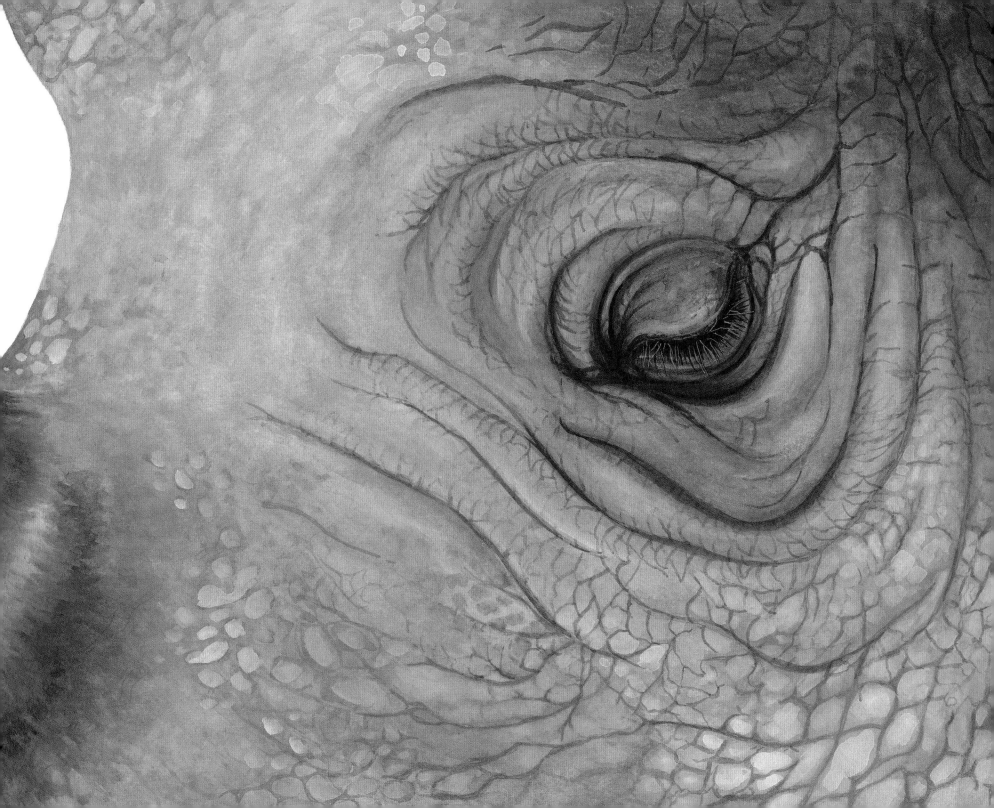

They sailed back to Holland, to the place from where Douwe himself had come. There the broad landscape was green, and life was quiet and peaceful. He built a fine stable for Clara and bought a large pasture for her to graze in. It had a little stream and a lovely mud hole. Clara bathed in the mud hole, ate the grass in the field, and was happy. Douwe came to see her every day. He would stand by the fence, and she would trot across so that he could stroke her head.

He would often talk to her about the exciting journeys they had made together and all the different people who had seen and admired her. Now it all seemed like a dream.

But the story is true. Clara's story is remembered even now. The pictures that were painted of her can still be seen in museums and art galleries today.

They tell of an age long past when once upon a time there was a famous rhino called Clara.

Author's Note The narrative begins shortly after the birth of Clara, which probably (about this there are no specifics) must have been in 1739. It is certain that Van der Meer bought Clara in 1741. It is believed that she could have been around for about two years at this time. The narrative in this sense includes the years of Clara's birth, 1739 to 1751, when Van der Meer returned to Leiden and stayed there for a few years (again, there are no exact details). I did not want to focus on the hardships that these trips might have caused Clara, although, of course, the possibilty remains that this was ultimately responsible for Clara's unexpected death. (If she had not previously been in good health, Van der Meer would not have made this trip to England with the precious animal.) In this respect, I chose not to end this story with her death. Therefore, my story ends at a time in Clara's life when Van der Meer's caring for the animal entrusted to him is in the foreground, thus placing the emphasis on the good relationship between them.—*Katrin Hirt*

Primary Source Material

Glynis Ridley, Clara's Grand Tour. The spectacular journey with a rhinoceros through Europe in the 18th century, Konkret Literatur, Hamburg, 2005.

(Original title: *Clara's Grand Tour: Travels with a Rhinoceros at Eighteenth-Century Europe*, Glynis Ridley, 2004.)

First published in the United States, Great Britain, Canada, Australia, and New Zealand in 2020 by NorthSouth Books, Inc., an imprint of NordSüd Verlag AG, CH-8050 Zürich, Switzerland.

Distributed in the United States by NorthSouth Books, Inc., New York 10016.

Library of Congress Cataloging-in-Publication Data is available.

ISBN: 978-0-7358-4395-0 (trade edition)

1 3 5 7 9 • 10 8 6 4 2

Printed in Latvia by Livonia Print, Riga, 2020.

www.northsouth.com

MIX
Paper from
responsible sources
FSC® C002795